The Fire Engine
Book & Puzzle Set

By Gail Herman
Illustrated by Carol Nicklaus

Learning Ladders/Random House

Bright and early at the firehouse, the day shift comes to work and the night shift goes home.

Roll call! The officer on duty takes attendance and then assigns each fire fighter a special job.

The day begins with housecleaning. The firehouse is like a home and everyone likes to keep it neat and clean. The fire fighters sweep the floors and make the beds.

They check that the fire trucks and all the equipment are in good shape. Are the axes sharp?
Are the air tanks filled?

Suddenly the alarm sounds. Bing-bing-bing!
The housewatch gets the call on a computer
and lets everyone know over the loudspeaker.
The fire fighters slide down the pole. *Wheeeee!*
They grab their fire coats, boots, and helmets
and jump into the trucks. Off they go!

KEEP BACK 500 FE

302

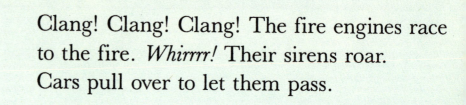

Clang! Clang! Clang! The fire engines race to the fire. *Whirrrr!* Their sirens roar. Cars pull over to let them pass.

There's the fire! *Screeeech!* The trucks scream to a halt. Flames lick the building. Thick black smoke billows out of its windows. Fire fighters jump off the pumper truck and quickly attach a large hose to the fire hydrant. They pump water into smaller hoses and then onto the fire. The crew from the ladder truck raises its ladder. Up they climb.

Crash! Fire fighters break open windows.
Whack! They cut holes in the roof. *Whoosh!*
Out rushes the smoke and heat.

The fire fighters check that everyone has left
the building. Some bring their hoses inside.
Chop! Chop! They cut down a fiery beam
with their axes. Rip! They pry up smoking
floorboards. At last the fire is out.

The fire engines drive slowly back to the station.
The officer writes a report about the fire.

The fire fighters talk about the fire.
They are happy that no one was hurt.
Then the fire fighters clean the trucks and the
hoses—and themselves. Everything must be
ready for the next fire.

It's been a busy morning, but now it's time for lunch. The fire fighters pile into their car to go food shopping. Just in case there's a fire, they can still be reached by radio and leave at a moment's notice.

Everyone helps prepare the meal.
The fire fighters are really like a family.

Now the fire fighters have some free time.
Some play chess or watch TV in the
recreation room. Others lift weights in
the gym. Some talk and relax, or study
the newest ways to fight fires.

Soon it's time for the night shift to come on duty. Their time is spent much like the day shift's. But when it starts to get late, the fire fighters bunk down to get some rest. That is, until the next fire alarm rings.